IT'S GOING TO BE

A BIG DAY

101 100-Word Stories by a 101-Year-Old

Eddy Goldfarb

Edited By

Lyn Goldfarb and Rene Goldfarb-Ilyashov

ISBN: 979-8-218-16540-6

LCCN: 2023904156

Table of Contents

STORIES OF MY LIFE 109

About the Author 130

Dedication

I am so happy to dedicate this book to my wonderful parents, my siblings Bernard and Bernice, my peacetime and wartime friends, my cherished wife Anita for 65 years of a loving marriage, my fantastic three children Lyn, Fran and Martin, my grandsons Rene and Guthrie, and my partner Greta.

But I don't want to forget Captain Wayne Merrill, skipper of my submarine, the Batfish. During World War II in the waters of the Pacific, we unexpectedly encountered the Japanese battleship Yamato, the world's biggest battleship, surrounded by what felt like millions of destroyer escorts. Captain Merrill reasoned that if we attacked the Yamato, we wouldn't be able to damage her enough to make it worth the cost of losing the submarine and the entire crew. He decided not to attack, and thanks to Captain Merrill, I'm still here today.

Introduction

Eddy Goldfarb is my father. He is one of the world's most esteemed toy inventors and a prolific writer of short stories. He is 101-years-old, and began writing when he was in his mid eighties. A man of passion, creativity, and ideas, he writes both fiction and non-fiction stories which illuminate his memories of his life, and offer insightful observations about living life to the fullest, love, and aging.

The child of immigrants, Eddy grew up during the Great Depression. During WWII, he volunteered for the Navy and served as a radar technician on the Batfish Submarine. In 1949, he sold the Yakity-Yak Teeth, the first of more than 800 classic toys over his 80-year career as an independent toy inventor. In 2003, Eddy was inducted into the Toy Industry Hall of Fame.

Eddy lives in a retirement community where he designs toys and other items in his garage machine shop, creates lithophane portraits on his 3D printer, and writes 100-word stories. In his story The Acorn 100-Word Contest, Eddy recalls how it all began.

Lyn Goldfarb

The Acorn 100-Word Contest

When I was eighty-six, I joined the contest that the *Acorn*, our neighborhood newspaper, ran every year. That is how I learned about the 100-word story which happens to be a popular hobby. I came up with this great story when I was about nineteen-years-old, but I never wrote it down. It was about an inventor who succeeded in printing a perfect counterfeit twenty-dollar bill. I thought it had a great surprise ending of how he was so easily caught.

No, I did not win the contest, but I caught the bug and have written more than 250 stories since.

January 2022

MY CHILDHOOD

My Earliest Memory

This is my earliest memory.

I don't think I was older than two, possibly even much younger. My parents bought me a "baby sit in," a very simple wooden rocking horse. I can still see it so clearly — two wooden sides, the upper part with the horse's head and body, the curved part on the bottom that allowed it to rock, a two-part seat in the middle, and finally, a bar in front for me to hold. They were trying to lift me into it and I screamed — I was terrified. They had to take it back to the store.

June 2017

My Father Brought Home a Radio

It was a very early model — a battery-operated radio. It was some time in 1926 and I was five years old. It was very exciting.

My father tried to make it work, but he finally gave up and handed the radio to me. It was the best toy I ever had. I couldn't make it work either, but I took it apart and closely looked at some of the parts. I learned what a battery was and I was able to make sparks by bringing the battery wire ends to almost touching. My interest in science took a giant step.

May 2017

My Number Four Erector Set

I do remember the two toys I played with when I was about six years old. The first was a metal truck and the second one was my favorite toy of all. It was an erector set with an electric motor. It was the one toy I really wanted and was thrilled when I received one for my birthday. I was so excited to play with it, but my older brother said he would show me how to play with it and he did, and he ended up taking it over and playing with it as much as I did.

January 2022

Five-Cent Soup Greens

That's what my mother often asked me to buy at the store on our block. Fresh greens and fine noodles. I was probably around seven years old and I didn't have to cross the street.

I still remember the clerk breaking off a piece of celery, one or two carrots, parsley, and some other vegetables. He rolled the vegetables up in wrapping paper.

My mother, of course, put the soup greens and chicken in a big pot to make chicken soup. When the soup was finished, she would remove the chicken and roast it in the oven. Both were great.

July 2017

My Father Loved the Canary

Bernard, my older brother who was sixteen, was selling clothes irons door-to-door to make some extra money. This lady wanted an iron and gave him a canary for it.

He brought it home in an empty clothes iron box. It was probably a sick bird because I remember the very sparse feathers around its neck. My father came home from work and loved the canary right away. He and Bernard went out and bought a cage for it, and the whole family gathered around the cage in the dining room. It was a very happy event and a good memory.

June 2017

Chief of the Police Boys

Please God, choose me. I prayed each time our teacher chose a new police boy. But the teachers never picked me. I was too short.

I ran for class president and lost, but was appointed police chief over all the police boys. But this didn't make up for not being selected.

I did some Navy shore patrol duty in San Francisco during WWII, but even that did not make up for the humiliation of never being a police boy — never standing at the crosswalk, helping students safely cross the street in front of my school, Volta Elementary in Albany Park.

August 2009

Freckles Day

My dad was sick in bed, but he gave my mother $5 so we could go to the Chicago World's Fair on "freckles day." That meant that both my freckled sister and I could get in for nothing. We kids had to go through a special entrance and meet my mother inside. We couldn't find her for hours, so we decided to see some of the attractions on our own while my mother hysterically tried to find us.

She finally found us after a couple of hours, but not before we saw the sensational Sally Rand, the fan dancer — WOW.

March 2021

My Chicago World's Fair Souvenir

My older brother, Bernard, worked at the 1933 Chicago World's Fair and brought home a souvenir for my sister and me. He gave me two shiny metal star badges with my name engraved on them, but only one was spelled correctly.

My younger cousin, Ronnie, who we all liked, was coming over. My mother thought he would be thrilled to have one of the badges. I agreed — and then my mother said it would not be nice if he got the one with the misspelled name. A discussion followed, and who do you think got the misspelled badge? You're right.

September 2009

Leo Stern

Leo Stern was my first really close friend. I was twelve and attending Volta Elementary School in Albany Park, Chicago. He was in my class and nothing more.

When my father died, my teacher mentioned it in class. Leo told his mother and she insisted that he bring me home — and that's how we became best pals. We were part of a group of school friends who hung around together, played sports, and bought five-cent hot dogs. But, I could not keep up with that crowd because I was always working, so my best friend became a very good friend.

December 2017

I Enjoyed Playing the Violin

I started violin lessons at eight and had to stop when I was twelve, after my father died. That meant a year of mourning — I had to stop playing the violin and, of course, leave the school orchestra. It wasn't that important to me because I knew that my music career in school was headed for bigger things.

In high school, I became the bass drummer in the ROTC band (that's another story), and when I went BOOM, pause, BOOM, pause, BOOM, BOOM, BOOM — the whole darn ROTC Corps started marching. My music career in school was a loud success.

November 2017

My Big Brother

My father died when I was twelve years old. My sister was ten and my brother was about nineteen. Our whole family structure changed — my brother became the father figure in our family.

When I had a problem, I went to him. He was great; he took his new status seriously. For example, when he and some friends went to the beach, he took me along. They all smoked. He insisted I smoke and I did. He made me smoke one cigarette after another until I got really sick. I will always be grateful to him. I never smoked again.

May 2017

My $2.00 Bad Memories

I had three unhappy school memories, all involving $2.00 — which was a lot of money back then.

The camping trip that my friends' fathers arranged cost $2.00. We couldn't spare the money, so I couldn't go.

There was a $2.00 deposit to use band instruments in my high school music class. I didn't have it, so I played the drum using a chair as a bass drum. In the end, it turned out great.

I had to drop out of night college because I didn't have $2.00 tuition, but I got a better job and was able to go back.

June 2017

My Pesty Sister's New Bike

My sister wrote that she was bringing home a new bike from Cleveland. Our relatives there had given her a present.

It was summer vacation and we all had to work, but we couldn't leave my sister home alone. My father's relatives in Cleveland sent for her and she had a wonderful vacation. They treated her royally and gave her a bike. I was glad for her, but envious.

l was so surprised to learn that my pesty little sister asked them to make it a boy's bike, so I could use it sometimes. Well, really, most of the time.

July 2015

Our Saturday Movie Day

It cost 10¢ each for my sister and me to watch a double feature. That's two complete movies and at least five shorts, including the news. And, of course, our weekly scary serial, which we eagerly looked forward to. They would even give away some prizes on stage. This all would take at least four hours. Sometimes, they passed out candy bars to get the kids to leave the theater, but we always stayed.

Then, my mom would come in with a bag of hot corned beef sandwiches for dinner and we would watch the whole darn thing over again.

February 2021

Wrestling with God

I was fifteen when I discovered girls…really one girl. I was struggling with the meaning of religion, life, the infinite universe, all that stuff, but mostly, is there a God?

And I saw Sheila — cute, smart, popular, hanging out in the crowd with the jocks. I knew I didn't have a chance.

Then it happened, she stopped me in the hall, just like that, and asked me to help her with her algebra homework. I was shaking, I practically yelled "Yes!" — and when she thanked me and touched my arm, I exploded and knew then there really was a God.

January 2009

My First Real Girlfriend

I was sick in bed when my sister introduced me to her friend from school, Siena Schwartz. She sat on my bed for the rest of the afternoon.

After that, we went steady for roughly two years. She was great and a real sport since I didn't have any money for normal dating. Eventually I broke it off, then she started it up again and I took her to her prom. The next day, she broke it off permanently.

We completely lost touch until I returned from WWII. You guessed it — I called, and a married woman answered the phone.

May 2017

My Best Friend Stole My Job

We were going to the cemetery to visit my father's grave, so I asked Penner, my best friend, to take my place as a soda jerk at Schuster's Drug Store. I was paying him and he had a wonderful time cleaning the soda fountain and polishing the soda glasses.

When I returned, the pharmacist who I didn't like, fired me and hired Penner. Penner happily took my place.

Later that evening, Mr. Schuster rehired me and fired Penner.

It wasn't because I was a better soda jerk, but because Schuster, "the mensch," knew I needed the job more — much more.

August 2018

My Haircuts

My brother was engaged to a very pretty and sweet girl whose father was a barber. He graciously gave us free haircuts in his apartment in the evening.

Meanwhile, my brother met another very pretty and sweet girl who he liked better. He finally had to break off his engagement to the first girl. He met up with her in the park and his new girlfriend sent me to spy on them from behind the bushes. We were all worried about how she would take the news. We were all very sad, especially me. That was my last free haircut.

June 2009

How I Got My First Name

ADOLPH, that's what my wonderful parents named me. They had no idea what I would go through with that name. We started hearing about Adolf Hitler when I was in my teens. I worked as a soda jerk at Schuster's Drug Store, and the guys who hung around there started calling me Eddie — and it stuck. I spelled it Eddie.

I wanted to join the Navy V7 radar program and took a special test from Captain Eddy in Chicago. I adopted the name EDDY and have used it to this day. I found out there are many men named Eddy.

November 2017

MY NAVY YEARS (WWII)

American Hospital, My Adventures

I studied and became a hospital medical laboratory technician at the American Hospital in Chicago. I felt it could support me while I studied physics.

In those days, you could become a hospital technician by studying and working in a hospital lab for about one year. I did the usual urinalysis, bloodwork, and pregnancy tests. I also worked with the pathologist doing microscope work and I helped with autopsies — but my specialty was pumping stomachs. The work was interesting and wonderful, but way too routine for me. So, when I joined the Navy, I just didn't tell them about it.

May 2017

I Never Fired a Gun

It's strange, I never fired a gun in World War II. In boot camp, they held up a rifle in front of about 200 of us and said, "This is a rifle." It was very early in the war and there just weren't enough weapons for everyone.

As a member of the crew on a submarine, you have to work very hard and learn every skill on the submarine. That's what makes you a qualified submariner. So, although I never fired a gun, I knew how to fire a torpedo, as well as how to perform dozens of other duties.

December 2017

How I Got Penner into the Navy

My friend, Penner, was upset, not just because the Navy rejected him, but that they accepted me on my second try. I was determined to help him. I was now serving at the naval recruitment area at the Great Lakes Recruitment Center. One of my jobs was to help the new recruits get their uniforms. My assignment was to stencil their name on their white pants. Penner applied once again, but this time I talked to the guy who was giving the eye tests and told him to pass him, and that is how we got Penner into the Navy.

May 2022

My Houston Movie Girlfriend

The Navy sent me to the University of Houston. I met this girl at the movies. She and her friend sat next to me, and we ended up dating for around three weeks. She was really hot, but I knew she had a boyfriend in the Army. While we were making out, she showed me his letter. She was using me to make him jealous, but I didn't care.

I remember the last line: "Of all the guys you could have gone out with, you picked a n***er loving, Yankee, Jewboy sailor."

I smiled as the letter hit the floor.

March 2009

Almost Shore Duty

I learned to control my stuttering in my senior year in high school. I lied about having a speech impediment when I joined the Navy. After the University of Houston and Treasure Island, I could have had shore duty, but I volunteered for submarines and was assigned to the new Batfish.

A week before sailing, I started stuttering in sound class. The admiral told my captain I couldn't go. I was devastated. My skipper told the admiral, "HE DOESN'T STUTTER WITH ME, HE'S GOING." I went, and I never stuttered again until my next relapse years later after the war.

January 2010

She Was the Prettiest at the Base Dance

No one asked her to dance. Why? This was my first dance at the Portsmouth Navy Yard. All the girls looked great, but she was the prettiest. Still, none of the other sailors asked her to dance.

I was bashful, but I took a chance and asked her to dance. She jumped up and then I knew why — one of her legs was twisted out of shape by polio. I wasn't a good dancer, but we got along fine and she was as nice as she was pretty, and I completely forgot about her leg. We had a great time.

June 2009

I Was Lucky

My skipper said, "You can't go to sub school in Key West, Florida. I want you here at the Navy Yard while the radar is being installed."

Most of the Batfish crew were new, had never submerged in a sub and would train on several old R class WWI subs in Florida. That week, the "R12" sank. All but 3 men were lost. The guys were assigned in alphabetical order. A friend's last name started with "H" — he was lost.

Years later, my wife and I started trips to Key West, but turned back for some reason each time.

September 2002

I Joined the Navy, the Song

"I joined the Navy to see the world, and what did I see? I saw the sea."

Exactly what I wanted. Because of my high marks at University of Houston and Treasure Island, I could choose my assignment, like teaching or being stationed in Washington. But I was very patriotic and wanted to show my appreciation to my country. I wanted to see action, no shore duty for me. So, I volunteered for sub duty with my buddies Erwin and Blackwood.

We saw the Pacific and the Atlantic and I did find them romantic, with a little action in between.

April 2010

Panama, Pepper Pot Soup, and Our First Action

I was eating Campbell's Pepper Pot Soup when the commotion started. A lookout had spotted a periscope sticking out of the water. On the surface, we were like any other surface vessel and just as vulnerable.

The OOD yelled, "Left full rudder, make ready two stern tubes." The captain rushed to the bridge, sounding the general alarm. He maneuvered the stern to face the Nazi sub's periscope and ordered, "Fire nine."

We spotted an air bubble, meaning they fired at us. Their torpedo wasn't sighted — they missed. And we missed. We left at flank speed, wondering if they got home.

September 2009

I Got Respect

Some of the regular crew members of the Batfish resented the fact that I was a first-class petty officer, not even serving for two years in the Navy. Some had to wait twenty years to achieve that rank.

Radar was new and very hush-hush.

But they loved us three radio tech guys when the SD radar detected the first low flying Japanese plane. With blinding sun behind the plane, the lookouts would not have spotted it with enough time for us to safely submerge before they reached us. Wow, did we get respect and encouragement to keep the radar running.

July 2017

The Great Lookouts on the Batfish

They were the lowest ranked crew members — they slept three to a bunk over the torpedoes.

We had the long-range radar to search for enemy ships. Our lookouts could see as far as the horizon, but they were also looking for periscopes sticking out of the water from submarines that wanted to sink us, and they did detect them.

Their reward: they were in the fresh air during the day and under starry skies at night while the rest of us, with higher ranks, were below decks for at least 75 days, no fresh air, sunny weather, or starry skies.

January 2018

Movie Time on the Batfish Submarine

The surface ships, when in port, showed movies on their decks at night. We showed our movies at sea, day or night, over and over again.

We had an 8 mm projector, a small screen, and one film for the whole patrol. There were 3 steps down into the forward torpedo room, and that's where five or six of us would sit — everyone, including the skipper. When there was no action, we took turns watching the movie. It was a Western and when we arrived at a sub base, we would trade the film with another sub…always for another Western.

November 2017

Howard McLarney's Dinner

Howard McLarney and I were transferred off the Batfish at the end of the fifth war patrol, to the Proteus, our mothership. Howard was going to be sent back to the states and assigned to a newly constructed sub, but would go on leave first. I was promoted to the Admiral's staff with no leave in sight.

Howard hated the food in the crew's mess. The food in the chief's mess was terrific and, after dinner, they put out a big ham and roast beef for snacks. Every night, I made Howard two huge sandwiches to keep him from starving.

November 2017

Last Night in Perth

It was our last night in Perth, Australia, and I was going out with my girlfriend Sandra. I really liked her and we saw each other every day since we docked.

McLarney, my best friend aboard the Batfish, pleaded with me to take him with us — he didn't want to be alone on our last night in Perth.

I did, and they fell in love. McLarney asked me to never write to her. He was my buddy, so I promised. Months later, she wrote to me saying she was sorry and wanted me to write.

But I kept my promise.

June 2009

The Good Old Days

During WWII on the Batfish submarine, I would climb down the hatch and not climb up to the surface for at least 60 days. No sunny days, no starry skies, enduring the worst kinds of stormy weather.

Planes bombed us, we were depth-charged hundreds of times. They fired their cannons at us, we fought on the surface with machine guns.

On our last night in Perth Australia, my best buddy Howard McLarney stole my new girlfriend.

Was it really the good old days? We were scared, but it was worth it.

You know why?

My shipmates…I miss my Batfish shipmates.

December 2021

I Had a Plan to End It

I was never that nervous during our numerous depth charge poundings — being an optimist helped. Our submarine would have to go deep below the surface to evade attacking ships above and I did formulate a plan, just in case.

If the explosions or the water depth ruptured the hull of the compartment I was in, water would rush in and I knew there was no chance I would survive. I figured out a plan. I didn't want to drown, so I thought I could knock myself out by hitting my head against one of the steel ribs in the compartment.

January 2011

Our President Has Died

I remember so well when President Roosevelt died. I was assigned to the Admiral's staff on our mothership, the Proteus, stationed at Guam. We were relaxing on deck when that sad announcement came over the intercom. It was unbelievable; we were in shock. It was as if every one of us had lost someone dear to us. Tears flowed — our Commander-in-Chief was only 63 years old. I was glad that he lived long enough to take charge of the events leading up to Nazi Germany's surrender. We owe so much to FDR for successfully steering us through those treacherous years.

December 2017

Batfish Retirement

January 2022

Is it just a tradition for submariners or is it all through the Navy? When the Batfish Submarine was retired to Muskogee, Oklahoma after the war, a bottle of Scotch was placed in a locker for the last one or two surviving crew members.

My daughter, Lyn, received a call from the Batfish Museum asking if we knew if other crew members were still around. This means they do not know if there are any other crew members except me at this time.

I hope I am not the last one and there are still others who are still afloat.

January 2022

TOY STORIES

Yakity-Yak Teeth

When I was first starting out as an inventor, I imagined someone could take out their false teeth and they would keep talking. I thought it was funny, so I made it happen.

But contrary to what people believe, I want to confess that I didn't invent real false teeth, only the Yakity-Yak Teeth which I hand carved.

I want to confess, contrary to what some people believe, I didn't invent false teeth. I just improved them.

Finally, I want to confess, contrary to what people may believe, I didn't invent real false teeth, I just made them YAK.

May 2011

Yakity-Yak Teeth: the Idea

I saw an ad in the paper for a tooth garage to store your false teeth. It gave me the idea to make a set of talking teeth. I went to my dentist and asked him for an old set of false teeth. I built a model using a windup motor. My associate knew Irving Fishlove, the novelty king, and we showed it to him. He loved it and bought it on the spot for $2500, but no royalties.

I was able to buy a Chicago winter overcoat.

It was 1949 and the last time I sold an invention outright.

December 2021

No Inventors Allowed

They would not allow inventors in the annual hobby show in Chicago, only toy buyers.

It was an important show and I came all the way from Los Angeles. I walked around the building and found an open door. It was dark and I realized I was behind the exhibits. I saw what I thought was a door and I pushed hard to open it and knocked down Ideal Toys' exhibit, really scaring the salesmen.

I apologized. They laughed it off and invited me to their headquarters.

Over the years, I ended up placing about fifty new toys with Ideal.

January 2022

Birth of the Merry-Go-Sip

I invented the Merry-Go-Sip because I knew mothers had problems getting their children to drink milk. If the child wanted the merry-go-round on top to go faster, they needed to drink more and more milk.

But I was just starting out, and making a workable model was challenging since I didn't own a lathe.

So, I converted my drill press into a vertical lathe to make the parts. Then I tested it. It was thrilling when the merry-go-round started turning faster and faster.

I now knew how Henry Ford must have felt when his first car started to move.

December 2022

My First Toy Show

My very first toy show in New York was truly a memorable event. I had three new items at the 1949 Toy Fair: the Yakity-Yak Teeth with Irving Fishlove & Company, and the Merry-Go-Sip and Busy Biddy with Topic Toys. They were all well received by the toy buyers. The New York press gave the show a lot of publicity and all three of my items were featured in newspaper stories. The toys were extremely successful when they finally hit the stores.

My wife, Anita, and I were very happy and very thankful for our newfound prosperity.

February 2018

Our Elvis Presley Gig

There are a few Elvis statues but the rarest one is ours because there is only one in existence.

Hank Saperstein, my associate in making Kellogg's premiums, was the licensing agent for Elvis. We knew Elvis well enough for my wife, Anita, to manage his fan mail. Hank and I decided to manufacture a small statue of Elvis. My friend, Tony Ballone, sculpted a terrific prototype and then we had a plastic company make the mold.

But it was a disaster. We got just one statue out of the mold.

That is why we have the rarest one of all.

February 2022

One-Way Ticket

Those early years of my toy inventing career were not always that great.

For example, a toy cap gun company in Pennsylvania liked one of my ideas, but I had to go there to close the deal. I only could afford a one-way ticket, but my wife, Anita, and I figured they would write the check right then.

They loved the item but could not send the check until the following week. So, I had to call my sister who sent me the airfare to get home.

They sent the check as promised and I paid back my wonderful sister.

January 2022

Stompers: the Beginning

It was Del Everitt, a fantastic industrial designer, who came up with the idea of making a toy version of the off-road, four-wheel drive trucks that were being introduced by the car companies. We liked the idea and decided to make small battery-operated miniature vehicles, but not exact copies. We would design them to be a little different, to look a little rougher and tougher, but still recognizable as the car model it was copied from.

As I remember, our first one was The Chevrolet Scottsdale K-10. We showed it to Bernie Loomis of Kenner Toys who bought the concept.

December 2022

Stompers: the Schaper Years

Several months later, Bernie Loomis returned the item because Kenner's R&D department screwed it up. And a few days after that, Bill Garrity, a newcomer to the toy industry walked in, hat in hand, with no money for an advance and in desperate need of a new item. He was really a banker who was taking over the Schaper Toy Company to save it from going bankrupt. We bonded. He needed all kinds of help.

I showed him the item — he liked it. I told him we would help him get the trucks to market. He named the line: Stompers.

December 2022

Stompers: Generation 2

Stompers were very successful. We concentrated on making new Stomper trucks, while Bill Garrity built the company back up. We did all the work for him on Stompers for a number of years. Del Everitt designed every new truck addition and we built new and exciting Stomper layouts. We did all the engineering.

While Stompers was already very successful, Norman Burger, my top model maker, made a huge improvement. He transformed our one-speed Stompers into two-speed, freewheeling Stomper trucks. Everyone loved the new design. It was like successfully introducing Stompers all over again and Norman got a nice fat bonus.

January 2023

My Bubble Gun

"Eddy, why would anyone pay four dollars when they could buy a bottle of bubble fluid for 39 cents?"

That was the reaction from every toy company when I showed my wonderful "bubble gun." I shelved the item, but later shared it with John Osher of Cap Toys and his girlfriend, Bonnie.

He said the same thing, but Bonnie disagreed, "John, you're going to make this item," and he said, "No, I am not. " And she said, "Yes, you are," and they went back and forth.

Finally, he said yes and it turned out to be a monumental success.

December 2021

My Vac-U-Form Toy

I was demonstrating my wonderful new toy vacuum form machine to Elliot Handler, the co-founder of Mattel Toys, when I noticed I was burning his desk. I used a light bulb instead of a heating coil to heat and soften the plastic sheet so it could be vacuum-formed over a pattern.

I was embarrassed, but he yelled, "DON'T WORRY ABOUT IT," as he hurried out to get Ruth, his wife and president of the company, to show her how the Vac-U-Form worked. They loved it and bought it on the spot and it became a big hit for many years.

April 2022

KerPlunk

We thought it was a promising idea, but we didn't know how successful the game would be. Rene Soriano came up with the original invention. I showed an excellent prototype to Ideal Toys. They licensed it on the spot, but none of us ever imagined it would become one of the best action games of all time.

The name KerPlunk originated with Ideal Toys and we were happy with the name and their commercials. To this day, it is very gratifying to hear from so many people, and now their own children, that they have happy memories playing the game.

June 2022

MY IMAGINATION: SHORT FICTION

Parallel Universes

I didn't agree with Professor Stephen Hawking's parallel universes theory, but maybe — hey, I'm getting ahead of my story.

My wife and I started our evening walk down our curved road to our neighbor's house. I went back for a jacket. It was only a minute, but when I rounded the bend, my wife wasn't there. My neighbors at the end of the curve didn't see her. We searched that night and the next day — no luck. But that evening, there she was, waiting for me, wondering why it took twenty minutes to get a jacket.

Maybe Stephen has something.

February 2009

Chess at Night

I live alone, but I play chess every night and morning against myself. My board is on the table next to my bed. I make one move at night and one in the morning and I generally remember my move from the previous night. So, it was kind of spooky when I noticed I made a move that I did not remember making. I tested this out by writing down my move the next evening and, sure enough, in the morning, I saw that a different move was made.

I don't know who my nightly opponent is, but he's winning.

March 2019

I Am a Garage Door Opener

You are amazed that I can speak and think. It's done differently, but we can do it. You humans see us as some sort of mechanical gadget, but the moment you finish manufacturing one of us and we can perform our task, we come to life.

I was born, created with a purpose. You see, having a purpose means you are alive. The opposite is also true. Being alive with no purpose is not really living. Every time you push the button, I do my job — opening and closing the garage door — and that's really living. It makes me happy.

September 2009

The Perfect Twenty-Dollar Bill

I did it. I finally succeeded in bleaching dollar bills for the blank paper. Now I was able to carry out the counterfeiting scheme I have been working on for years.

I took a twenty-dollar bill from my wallet and took it through the process. It was a perfect copy. To test it, I used it to pay for a hamburger and the next thing I knew I was arrested.

How did the kid at the counter detect it? I was going crazy. The detective sneered as he explained that I "made a perfect copy of a lousy counterfeit bill."

March 2009

My Boss

I found my soulmate, my Irish rose, the one I will love forever and she really loves me. We are going to get married, but we have to tell her dad. He is everything to her, especially after her mom died.

But, he's my boss. He's tough; his name is O'Reilly. We're so different. My name is Goldberg, I went to his office shaking and told him about us. He stared at me and quietly said, "I need a drink." He poured two. I was in shock when he held his up, looked at me, winked, and said quietly, "L'chaim."

November 2008

Supermarket Drama

It really happened, I was the supermarket cashier on the late shift and I saw everything. It was nice, I mean, really nice.

They each had a cart and were shopping for what they normally needed. She was going her way and he was going his, when — boom — they ran into each other while reaching for the pancake mix. They apologized to each other and talked for a while. Soon they were shopping side by side.

I knew it was a done deal when they came to the checkout counter with just one basket filled with what they both liked.

September 2009

Sad and Happy

She was lonely and sad.

She had some friends, but no one really close and no romantic interest. The pandemic didn't help; she was really frightened and stayed home a lot. She ordered all kinds of things on the internet and so looked forward to receiving the many packages. Every day, she was excited to greet the mailman, who had her newest purchases in hand. But you know, if you looked in her closet, most of them sat there unopened.

I think most of you really know what happened next. You're right.

She ended up happy.

She married the mailman.

January 2021

My Dad Was a Writer

Not really, my dad was an insurance man. But writing short stories was his hobby and we loved them. We encouraged him to try to get them published, but they never were.

Dad was seriously ill and we knew we were going to lose him at any time. I went for the mail while mom and sis stayed with him. There it was — a publisher's letter accepting his story.

I ran upstairs yelling, "Dad, your story was accepted." His eyes fluttered open, looked at us, and then closed. We all were in tears, but happy, sure that he had heard.

December 2017

Up, Up and Away

They cut the ropes and he was going up, higher and higher into the sky. His dream of flying with hundreds of party balloons attached to his chair was finally happening. Ever since he read about the flying man, Larry Walters, he knew that someday he would do it, too. The wind on his face felt so good.

They found him in the morning. He passed on in his sleep. He seemed so peaceful, looking at the get-well helium balloons tied to his bed. They were gently bobbing up and down with a slight breeze from the barely open window.

December 2008

I Just Knew it Was Henry

There was a spider in the bathroom and I thought, "That's really Henry."

We lost Henry months ago when he speedily drove into a tree. It reminded me of those evenings when we played that old game, the one where we talked about which animal we would want to be in our next life. There were plenty of kittens and puppies, but Henry, my brother-in-law, wanted to be a spider. I thought it suited him because of the way he treated my sister — captured her in his web.

I'm not afraid of spiders, but I just stepped on him anyway.

May 2017

Tahiti

Dad is 78, Mom, 72. Dad is ok, but Mom has some health problems. He takes good care of her.

I told them, "It's time for me to know more about your financial and medical details — just in case, you know, Dad, you may go off to Tahiti someday." I was joking of course, but we all understood.

A week later, Mom called, crying and shrieking, "Dad went to Tahiti." I screamed that my dad was dead, and it started to sink in.

"Where's my daddy?" I screamed.

Mom waved around a note yelling, "The old bastard went to Tahiti."

November 2011

A Narrow Escape

We were on the way to our vacation hotel. It was late and raining hard, when all of a sudden, we saw headlights coming at us fast, and in our lane. I don't know how we managed to miss the car — our hearts were still pounding when we reached our hotel. Our room was radiantly beautiful and my favorite red cherries were on the table.

My husband exclaimed, "Hey, yellow cherries! They're the best."

I said, "No, they're red." He started to say yellow when he reached out and held me.

I whispered, "We didn't miss the car, did we?"

August 2009

My Buddy

Have you ever thought you saw someone who is no longer with us, someone who so resembled that person, that it really startled you?

It happened to me. We were shipmates in WWII. I was lucky, he wasn't. He didn't make it back.

I was so startled when I thought I saw him at the mall. Of course, I knew it was just someone who looked like him, but I followed him anyway. He went up the escalator and at the top, walked off into the crowd. Except, you know, before he disappeared, he turned around and waved at me.

October 2019

L.G.O.

In the 3rd house from the corner, they gathered in the bedroom around his bed. Nick was dying. He was surrounded by his family who loved him. He was a decent guy, a good father and husband — and he was going to be missed. He was 90 and lived an active life, but he missed his wife who passed 11 years ago.

In the distance, you could hear the sound of garbage cans being emptied. Listening closer, you could have even been able to hear the cries of a newborn baby in the house at the end of the block.

February 2020

THE GOLDEN YEARS

Dating an Eighty Five Year Old

I remember when I was your age, I also asked and wondered why anyone would ever think about dating a lady who is eighty- five. But you will realize, as the years roll by and you are also getting older, that the ladies are still wonderful, smart, exciting, and beautiful — and still able to turn you on. Oh sure, there are wrinkles and she may not stand up so straight, or she may be lugging around a walker or cane.

Who would want to date an eighty-five-year-old woman? I will tell you who………….lot of ninety-year-old men, that's who.

April 2019

Making Out When You Are Old

It doesn't have to be all over when you're old. Of course, you have to slow down a little, take things easier, and learn to play the game.

Old age romance, that's what I'm talking about. Friendship is great, but mixing in a little warmth really helps. Holding hands, hugging, and even a good night kiss — they can help your heart and all the rest of your bodily functions.

But you have to be very careful, all this could lead to something you didn't expect. Something hard to handle, something that may worry your kids.

It could lead to dancing.

October 2018

Guys, Gals, We Are Getting a Little Older

Getting older doesn't mean it's all over for us. It's healthy and normal to have that same old feeling for wonderful people who also feel it's not over for them.

You can court each other in so many exciting and warm ways, not necessarily for marriage, but for close friendships — really close, if you know what I mean.

We are no longer interested in how good looking someone is or what their prospects are, as long as they are a nice person. But there is one new criterion that is really very important: make them laugh...make them laugh...make them laugh.

October 2018

CO₂X

My wife and I love the seltzer that we make ourselves using a device that infuses CO_2 into water. The CO_2 cartridges come from a small company in Florida. The salesman encouraged us to buy the CO_2X brand at three times the cost because it has a little something extra — no one knows what, but he insisted that we'd like it.

We enjoyed the seltzer so much that our evening ended up turning into something special, if you know what I mean. Now, when we yell, "Seltzer!" it's not necessarily because we're thirsty — again, if you know what I mean.

May 2012

Sorry for Your Loss

They gathered at the house after the funeral. Gerald fondly greeted the mourners. He was seventy-ish, looking very well. It was a good marriage and he is successful in real estate.

Emma introduced herself, expressing her sorrow, and explained that she knew his wife in college. They were wonderful friends, but lost touch. He responded warmly and guided her to a blonde woman who also told him that she, too, was an old college friend. The women greeted each other. Once Gerald left, Emma looked her straight in the eye, murmuring, "You didn't know her either."

She meekly nodded yes.

January 2009

My New Neighbors

I remember as a young boy that when a new family moved into our apartment building, I was always excited hoping that there would be a boy my age that I could play with.

As you grow older, having your own family and living in places for longer periods of time, you still are kind of curious about the new people that are moving in down the block or even next door.

So, even now, I was curious about the new neighbors moving in across the street and was kind of disappointed because it's just another couple of old people.

February 2021

The Tennessee Waltz

When I visited my mother at the Alzheimer's Center, I would see them dancing so beautifully and always to the "Tennessee Waltz." She is a patient and he really is her husband who visits her every day. Her memory is gone and he doesn't want to upset her, so on every visit, he introduces himself as a new friend and asks her to dance. They always dance to the "Tennessee Waltz" and they are very good.

When asked, she explains he is a special new friend, someone she can trust and he so reminds her of her late dear husband.

November 2013

Seventy Years

We didn't see each other for seventy long years, but he called after Dick died. We were both close friends of Dick and we were very competitive. It was exciting — it felt as if we were the only survivors of those high school years.

Each of us claimed we were doing and feeling great and made a date for lunch. We had a wonderful lunch and reunion. As I slowly walked out, I noticed the wheelchair outside the doorway and I knew why he didn't get up. I, in turn, hoped he wouldn't notice my walker and attendant waiting outside.

August 2009

Her Scream Woke Me

I woke from a deep sleep. It was a shrill scream, full of fear. I held her hand and soothed her, telling her it was only a nightmare, until she fell back to sleep. How could I leave her? I can't, she is so frail, especially at times like this.

I will do everything the doctors prescribe, even though the odds are against me. I will take the treatments. I will exercise, and above all, I will be more positive. I will never leave her. I will get well — and I did. The doctors agreed it was a miracle recovery.

September 2009

Someone Is in My Bed

It was 4:00 in the morning when I was awakened by breathing sounds in my bedroom. I was shaking with fear when I realized they were coming from my own bed.

But the sounds somehow soon calmed me. They were low, soothing, happy sighing, sleeping breaths — like the soft voice of a happy woman. Suddenly, I wasn't afraid. They were comforting sounds and I soon fell asleep. I awoke the next morning totally refreshed and smiling about my dream. I have slept alone these past four years since my wife passed away — I know I won't be alone again tonight.

June 2009

Shuffle Along, the Musical

Great show song; the music is great. But for anyone over the age of seventy…

The message is WRONG.

Don't shuffle, never shuffle. It makes you look old and if you are already old, it makes you look a lot older.

The only time you should ever shuffle is when you are wearing house slippers that are too big and you shuffle to keep them from falling off. That's it, no other time.

Keep your head up high, shoulders back, tuck it in, and walk with a smile on your face,

But for goodness sake, watch where you are going.

May 2019

Cookies and Cream Pie

Listen, I understand, you don't have any more cookies-and-cream pie. That happens once in a while, maybe I can get it next time. Of course, I was looking forward to it — it's my favorite pie — but you know you can't have everything in life. Thank goodness I'm still here. Ok, a dish of prunes will be fine. It's a healthy dessert. Worse things have happened to me, like going through this virus business — staying at home with nothing to do, hardly seeing anyone, having to wear masks.

But thanks for calling, I'm ok. I should have ordered the cheesecake.

October 2020

Who's Whom

Our friends, Sheila and Joe, happily told us about the beautiful new cat they acquired two weeks ago, but they have not seen it since. They put out food and water on their balcony every morning which the cat clearly enjoys and they also tend to the litter box, but no cat has ever been seen.

I laughed hysterically when I realized that they think they welcomed a warm and cuddly pet into their home, but in actuality, the cat took over a nice apartment with a balcony and two kind elderly humans who take care of its every need.

August 2020

Let Them Wait

The young are just not up to it – getting old.

They lack so many qualities and experiences that would truly identify them as old people. Most — thankfully — are not that interested. But there are some who long for the serenity, peacefulness, and feeling of accomplishment of a job well done. Actually, they know relatively little about life, but why should they know more? They lack the actual time it takes to get old and the layers of life a person climbs through to truly become old.

They should be satisfied with their youth and let time do its noble work.

July 2010

I Want to Be an Old Guy

"I want to be an old guy just like you, Grandpa."

That's what my grandson answered when I asked him what he wanted to be when he grew up. "I want to sleep late, play cards with your friends, and have a good time — just like you."

I told him it's not easy to do. You have to study hard, love and respect other people, be a loyal friend, work at something you love, and be an all-around decent human being. It takes a great deal of effort and a lot of years, but I know you can do this.

December 2010

She Looked Sad

I usually saw her once or twice a week on my morning walk. We would say hello and maybe exchange a few more words in passing. It bothered me that she always looked sad and hardly smiled.

One day, I decided I would try to cheer her up by telling her a joke the next time we met — and I did. She smiled, laughed, and told me it was cute. But, most importantly she said, "It was a nice way to start the day." And you know, it was really a nice way for me to start my day, too.

At Her Age

It's unbelievable, her mom is a hundred years old and a great grandmother, and asking her daughter if, at her age, is it proper to be more than friends with this guy at her retirement village?

She reminded her mom. "You are both by yourselves with no commitment with anyone else. Of course, it is ok. It's like having a last fling." She assured her mom that her family approves. In addition, they all know about him and like him. He is just one year older than she is, and most important of all, he is a nice Jewish boy.

December 2022

STORIES OF MY LIFE

How I Met Your Mother

Hank and I went to this dance. I was sitting when they walked by. I noticed her tush and then her face — it was wow! Not just because she was beautiful, but behind those blue eyes, there was so much more. The first things I asked were: was she single and did she have a job? Kidding, those are TV lines.

We danced and when I held her and she wrinkled her nose, that was it. I didn't want to rush her or look like a weirdo, so I waited until the next day to ask her to marry me.

October 2018

I Am Not Superstitious

Absolutely not, I don't believe in that superstition nonsense — but I do create simple good luck routines to make me feel better. For example: my yellow underwear shorts.

For years, when I traveled by plane, I wore yellow underwear shorts. I believed that if I wore them, I would have a great flight. As time went on, it didn't really matter if I actually wore the underwear — I knew that I had some at home. After years of wear, they disappeared. But I knew that yellow underwear shorts existed somewhere in the world, so I would have a safe flight.

May 2011

My Three WWII Caps

Years ago, my doctor told me to wear a cap for sun protection. My wife, Anita, designed a World War II cap and had three versions of it made over the years. So many people have seen me wearing the cap and thanked me for my service during World War II.

At one event, a man approached me from behind, pushed a $100 bill into my hand and left before I could see his face. Another time, a nice lady wanted to buy me dinner and offered me $20. I thanked her and laughingly told her that it wasn't enough.

February 2018

The Best Chinese Dinner

We finished our excellent dinner at this, new for us, Chinese restaurant when I discovered that both my wife, Anita, and I left our wallets at home. I was embarrassed and I told the cashier who said she understood. She said it can happen to anyone and told me to wait. I thought she was speaking to the manager, but no, she came back to tell me that the cook and herself were going to pay my check and I could come back sometime in the next few days to pay them back.

That really was our best Chinese dinner.

December 2017

The Cats that Wave at You

We stopped in Singapore and went sightseeing in Chinatown. One shop had these waving good luck cats. They were motorized and could wave continuously for several months on one battery. I was fascinated. They were cheap and could make great gifts. I bought one dozen. Back home I arranged them on a shelf, what a sight. I ordered more, a lot more, what wonderful gifts.

I can't count how many I have now all over the house, all waving. No, I haven't given any away yet, but I'm going to. This afternoon I'm bringing one to my shrink, shrink, shrink.

November 2008

An Old Joke

I was getting an estimate from my auto mechanic. It was too high and I stalled answering. He was very interested in seniors — and of course, I am one.

He asked about my health, activities, and wife — especially curious about if we were still doing it. I told him, of course, we try four or five times a week. He was speechless. I told him we try on Monday; if nothing happens, we try on Tuesday; if nothing happens, we try again on Wednesday — as in the joke.

He didn't get it. But he did lower the price a lot.

November 2009

A 3D Printer Is a Calming and Soothing Influence

Owning and using a 3D printer is very healthy for you.

Of course, there are some precautions you must take, like having your printer in a well-ventilated room or in an enclosure. Making, creating, or building something from zero, from the very beginning and watching it grow into something meaningful, is very pleasant and rewarding. It's like planting magic flower seeds in a pot and seeing beautiful flowers grow in hours instead of weeks. It's like baking a cake or roasting a turkey in the oven. Your brain is stimulated. This results in positive feelings in all your body functions.

November 2022

Bathroom Lock-Up

My wife, Anita, and I were on a cruise and stopped at this exotic island. We and our friends visited this little museum, when I had to go to the men's room. Someone took me to a little building with a toilet. When finished, I realized I was locked in and the ship was leaving soon. I had a knife and frantically carved a hole around the lock and got out.

I often wondered if Anita and the others would have returned or sailed away without me if I did not escape from my toilet prison. What do you think?

January 2022

Bathroom Lock-Up 2

After my heroic escape from the toilet building, I joined Anita and our friends and hurried back to the ship before it would pull up anchor and leave. I was still wondering if they would have left without me, so I came right out and asked Anita. She laughed and said, "Of course, we would have waited for you. I am your wife and I love you; you are the father of our great kids and, of course, the most important reason of all, you were wearing the money belt that had all our cash and return home airline tickets."

January 2022

Marvin

My wife, Anita, and I met Marvin and Lonnie when they moved to the island in Westlake Village many years ago. They lived a few channels from us. We became very friendly and took many wonderful trips together. We stayed good friends through the years. When Anita and I decided to retire to University Village, they followed us there.

Marvin enjoyed playing poker and that helped a lot after he lost Lonnie.

You might say that life is a little like a poker game and Marvin lost that last hand, but I do not think so; I think he won.

April 2022

It's Beshert (It's Destiny)

"It's been planned," the very wise lady says.

Greta, of course, is talking about our getting together so unexpectedly, a surprise. But there it is, as if we were given another chance at youth. It's got to be nurtured very carefully. It's so wonderful, but delicate — it can be shattered and ruined by rushing in, instead of threading softly and slowly. All the while, we laugh, love, and enjoy every step of the way.

How fortunate can we be? There is so much heartache in everyone's lives. How lucky I am, to be lovingly guided by this very wise lady.

August 2013

My Significant Other Is a Neat Freak

Being neat is a wonderful trait. I certainly admire her for that, especially since I am the exact opposite.

A most successful and extremely happy relationship can still be had if both parties listen and respect each other's mishigas.*

An extreme example:

Before my sweetie leaves home, the entire house must be clean and everything in its place. The reason is simple: what if she doesn't come back, what would people think of her?

My reasoning is the exact opposite. You leave the piles of stuff, so you must come back before anyone has a chance to view your mess.

(*mishigas means craziness)

April 2017

Falling Back to Sleep

Like most of us, you may have had the kind of bad night when you wake up in the middle of the night feeling very low and can't go back to sleep. I have found that the best thing for me is to get up and do something, like cleaning up a pile of stuff or even answering some emails. In other words, accomplishing something that you have avoided. If you can do something creative, that's even better. And then, go back to sleep.

You will wake up to a bright, wonderful, promising new day — even if it's raining outside.

March 2019

Oh, to Be Eighty Again

Do you believe that if you wish hard enough, some of your wishes can really come true? But you must be a little sensible and practical about what you wish for. If you want a million dollars, be reasonable and start with just $100,000 and work up.

I want to go back to my younger days, but again, I do not want to ask for way too much. Not to my high school days. I just want to go back to when I was eighty, when I was surrounded by so many people who were near and dear to me.

July 2022

The Secret of Life

June 2022

I found that as I grew older, into my nineties, there are even more questions to the age-old questions, "what is life all about, why, and how?" I realized that there were clues. And the older I got, the more clues there were.

Finally, when I hit that really big birthday, it all came together, and I was so privileged to learn the answers to all my questions and they were so beautiful. I was happily relieved.

I know you're anxious for me to tell you all about what I know, and I really want to...if only I could remember.

A Great One Hundred Years and Still Going

My dad died when I was twelve — our lives changed completely. We worked together and made it. World War II started; I joined the Navy, volunteered for submarine duty, and was assigned to the Batfish, saw lots of action. Fortunate to come home, I met Anita, my wonderful wife and partner for sixty-five years, had three wonderful children, two grandsons. I was very successful inventing hundreds of toys. We traveled the world. We live in California, and now in University Village retirement area. I lost Anita, tied up with Greta — and in two hours, my 100th birthday. I made it!

September 4, 2021 (10 pm)

Come to Think About It

I can't remember anyone who was one hundred years old before we moved to University Village, so maybe it's something special. My kids thought it was, my little sister thought it was (she is ninety-eight), my movie group friends here at the Village — who gave me a wonderful party — thought it was, but not me. It is just another birthday and, of course, I am looking forward to many more. I now realize it is something special and I am really grateful. But I miss so many that I loved — that were dear to me — and often wonder, why me?

October 2021

101 Years Old

Becoming 101 years old brought me some extra attention. Both family and friends were excited about this big birthday. I pretended that it was just another birthday, nothing to be that excited about.

Some of my younger friends even threw me a party which was great — and I had a wonderful time. One of my friends, who is in his early eighties, said he hoped he could make it to a 101 as well.

I told him, "Don't worry, just keep doing what you are doing. In fact, you look like you're 98 now, so you're well on your way."

October 2022

It's Going to Be a Big Day

Every day when I wake up, I thank him, her, or it for this wonderful new day.

Before I go to sleep at night, I usually go over the events of the day in my head and review the problems I encountered in my work.

During the night, everything becomes much clearer and even some of yesterday's problems are solved.

I sometimes think that I get a little help, perhaps from family and friends who are no longer with us.

Rain or snow, cloudy or sunny, we are given a new, wonderful opportunity.

It's going to be…A BIG DAY.

August 2018

About the Author

Eddy Goldfarb was born in 1921 in Chicago, Illinois; the son of Jewish immigrants from Poland and Romania. His birth name was Adolph. He was one of three children — Bernard was five years older and Bunny (Bernice) was two years younger.

Even as a young child, Adolph was interested in how things work. He recalls that when he was around five years old, his father, Louis, brought home an early radio and when it didn't play, he gave it to Adolph to take apart to see how it worked. He remembers that it was one of the best toys he ever had.

Louis worked as a tailor in a garment factory, and sold goods on a pushcart on Maxwell Street to make extra money. Louis died in 1933 at the young age of 44 and Adolph's life changed dramatically. He was 12 years old, and along with his brother, and mother, Rose, they worked to support the family.

Money was always scarce, but Adolph did his part. He delivered newspapers and groceries. One of his best jobs was working as a soda jerk for Schuster's Drug Store. And it was there that his friends stopped calling him Adolph (in reaction to Adolph Hitler's rise to power) and started calling him Eddie. He later changed the spelling to Eddy, after taking a Navy radar exam from Captain Eddy.

Eddy excelled in math and science in high school, and was interested in studying physics, but he knew college would have to wait until he could afford the tuition.

A big turning point in Eddy's life was World War II. When Pearl Harbor was bombed, Eddy enlisted in the Navy. As the child of immigrants, he was very patriotic and wanted to give back to the country that welcomed his parents. He enrolled in a special program to learn about radar.

The Navy sent him to the University of Houston where he studied electrical engineering, and later to a secret lab on Treasure Island in San Francisco Bay to specialize in radar.

As a radar technician, Eddy volunteered for submarine duty and was assigned to the Batfish Submarine. It was still under construction, and he was on the first crew to take it out to sea. He served in the Navy for 3 ½ years.

At the end of his 5th war patrol, he was promoted to Chief Radio Technician and assigned to the Admiral's staff on the mothership, the Proteus.

When Eddy began his service on the Batfish, he was allowed to bring only one sea bag onboard, and he filled it with clothing, books, and a spool of magnetic wire which he used to build tiny motors. While at sea, Eddy invented a specialized radar antenna. He also had a sketchbook and he made drawings of his inventions.

When the war in Europe ended, Eddy started thinking about his future. He knew he wanted to be an independent inventor, and realized he needed to specialize. He looked for an industry that was open to new ideas and didn't require a lot of money to begin inventing. He chose toys.

After the war, Eddy returned to Chicago where he met Anita, who he proposed to the day after he met her at a dance, and they were married nine months later in 1947. Anita agreed to support Eddy for two years while he pursued his dream to become an independent inventor.

The first toy he sold was the Yakity-Yak Teeth, a simple gag item which became a cultural icon. He partnered with promoter Marvin Glass, and they brought the Yakity-Yak Teeth to novelty king Irving Fishlove. Eddy kept inventing, working day and night, coming up with new ideas, and making the models himself.

In 1949, Eddy had 3 toys at the Toy Fair in New York, the toy industry's annual showcase: Yakity-Yak Teeth (Fishlove), Busy Biddy Chicken (Topic Toys), and Merry-

Go-Sip (Topic Toys). All three toys were big hits and Eddy's career was launched.

Eddy always wanted to live in California and in 1952, Eddy, Anita, and their 2-year-old daughter, Lyn, moved to Los Angeles. Marvin was angry that Eddy moved to California and refused to send Eddy any of the royalties that were owed to him. While California represented a new start, Eddy and Anita had a tough time financially. They moved into a modest home in the San Fernando Valley and Eddy set up a model shop in their one-car garage.

Times were so difficult that when their daughter, Fran, was born in 1953, Eddy didn't have enough money to pay the hospital bill. He recalls that he went to the home of Lew Glaser of Revell Toys that night with a new toy idea and walked out with a check, allowing him to pay the bill and bring Anita and their new daughter home.

By the time their son, Martin, was born in 1957, Eddy's business had grown. He soon outgrew his shop in the garage, and at the height of his success, Eddy owned 3 buildings and employed 39 people — model makers, industrial designers, engineers, sculptors, and support staff.

Eddy designed a wide range of toys, games, novelties and hobby kits for boys and girls of all ages. He invented more than 800 toys and holds close to 300 patents. Some of his most successful toys were: Yakity-Yak Teeth, Battling Tops, Vac-U-Form, Arcade Basketball, KerPlunk, Hydro Strike, Giant Bubble Gun, Baby Beans, Stompers and Shark Attack. He sold toys to most of the toy companies in the U.S. and branched out to Europe and Asia.

He had a particularly close working relationship with two of his designers, his associate Del Everitt, for Stompers, and Rene Soriano, for KerPlunk. In 1998, Eddy formed a new partnership with his son, Martin, (the inventor of Shark Attack). And to this day, Eddy & Martin Goldfarb and Associates are continuing to invent toys and games.

In 2003, Eddy was inducted into the Toy Industry Hall of Fame and in 2010, received the TAGIE (Toy and Game Innovation) Lifetime Achievement Award from the Chicago Toy and Game Group. He was the first American to receive the I.D.I.O.T. (International Designer and Inventor of Toys) at the London Toy Fair in 1993.

In addition to Eddy's career inventing toys, he worked with Hank Saperstein to design and manufacture toy premiums for Kellogg's Cereal, and they worked with Elvis Presley to create an Elvis plastic figurine (which was never released). As part of their collaboration, Anita answered Elvis's fan mail. Eddy also designed spy devices and gadgets for the 1960s TV show, "The Girl from U.N.C.L.E." In 1985, Eddy was one of first inventors to venture into video games (Epyx Barbie and Epyx Hot Wheels, both with Mattel) but chose not to continue, focusing instead on his passion — designing toys and games.

Eddy now lives in a retirement community, where he has transformed his garage into a machine shop. He still designs new toys and creates assistive devices to help seniors. He is a collector of porcelain lithophanes (19th century translucent pictures) and now creates his own lithophane photographs on his 3D printer. He is a prolific writer of short stories, specializing in 100-word stories, which capture the stories of his life and the fiction of his imagination. He exercises and walks every day.

In 2013, Anita, Eddy's wife of 65 years died, and he is now in a relationship with Greta, who also lives in the retirement community.

Eddy turned 101-years-old on September 5, 2022.